My Blissful Experiences with Life!

Copyright Page

My Blissful Experiences with Life!

ISBN: Paperback / Softback: 978-93-343-2891-2

E-book reader: 978-93-343-3346-6

Publisher Information: Paremvir Malik Address: Flat No.304, 2nd Floor, Whitehouse Apartment, RZB-1A, KHASRA NO.358-207, Nr. Shiv Mandir Chowk, Vill - Masoodpur, Vasant Kunj, New Delhi - 110070, INDIA

Author Details: Paremvir Malik

Website/Contact Information:

LinkedIn: https://www.linkedin.com/in/paremvir/

Email: paremvir@gmail.com

Disclaimer

The information provided in this book is for general informational and inspirational purposes only. It is not intended to be a substitute for professional advice, whether medical, psychological, financial, or otherwise. The author and publisher make no representations or warranties of any kind, express or implied, about the completeness, accuracy, reliability, suitability, or availability with respect to the book or the information, products, services, or related graphics contained in the book for any purpose. Any reliance you place on such information is therefore strictly at your own risk.

Edition Information: First Edition

Cover Design Credits: My Daughters Aishwarya (Princess) and Shaurya (Oyu) Malik

Dedication

To Life, my eternal Mother, my profound Guru, my steadfast Friend, my demanding yet fair Hard Taskmaster, and my awesome Mentor in all phases. May this book reflect the profound journey of learning, growth, and heartfelt understanding.

Acknowledgements

Writing a book is often a solitary journey, yet it's profoundly supported by the love and understanding of those around us. My deepest gratitude goes to my sweetheart wife, Shilpi, and my sweet twin daughters, Princess (Aishwarya) and Oyu (Shaurya). Your immense support, patience, and understanding while I was engaged in writing this book were invaluable and truly made this endeavor possible.

Special Thanks to my friends Ayush for proof reading english version and mountain of valuable suggestions, Ms. Himanshri Chaudhary (Founder - Himanshri Success School) for her motivating followups for release of English Version Manuscript and proof reading of upcoming Hindi version of the book expected to be released by mid 2026.

Once again, A BIGGGG THANK YOU to all those who motivated and made this dream come true !

Gratitude, Paremvir

Table of Contents

Introduction: My Journey to Bliss

Since childhood, I've harbored a profound fascination with human behavior, especially the intriguing question of "Why do they do, what they do?" This innate curiosity has been a guiding light throughout my life. Thus, I became naturally observant and contemplative while studying human behavior, and this led to better insights as I grew older. I gradually developed a hobby of crafting these insights in the form of short quotes.

My professional journey as a Human Resource leader further added immense value to these insights and refined them significantly. Finally, after 10 years of writing my quotes, I decided to compile them in the form of this book and in future editions. This book, "My Blissful Experiences with Life!", is a culmination of these lifelong observations and the humble insights gathered along this journey.

I sincerely hope these quotes will prove helpful to my readers, making their lives more blissful and prosperous.

Section 1:

The Inner Compass

Thoughts on Self-Awareness & Truth

Quote 1:

*"Mind is selfish, Heart is emotional... the soul speaks the Truth,
listen to it always!"*

Our mind often gravitates towards self-interest, while our heart is swayed by emotions. However, beneath these layers, our soul possesses an unwavering connection to universal truth. By consciously tuning into this inner voice, we can navigate life's complexities with clarity and integrity. Listening to the soul is key to authentic decision-making.

Space for Self Contemplation Notes !!!

Quote 2:

"Perceptions seed illusionary misunderstandings, but grow real pain... watch your mind!"

Our interpretations of events can often create a false sense of understanding, leading to imagined conflicts. Despite being rooted in illusion, these misunderstandings can manifest into genuine emotional distress and conflict. It's crucial to be mindful of our perceptions, as they directly influence our emotional well-being and relationships. Cultivating objective thinking helps prevent unnecessary suffering.

Space for Self Contemplation Notes !!!

"The way you feel from inside reflects in your smile on the outside!"

Our inner emotional state has a profound impact on our outward expressions, especially our smile. A genuine smile originates from a place of true happiness and contentment within. Conversely, a forced smile often betrays an inner struggle or lack of joy. This quote signifies that true outward radiance stems from inner peace and authenticity.

Space for Self Contemplation Notes !!!

Quote 4:

"A blunder is when you lie to yourself... Heart revolts eventually!"

Lying to oneself, whether through self-deception or ignoring inner truths, is a grave mistake that has deep consequences. While we might temporarily escape external judgment, our conscience and inner being will eventually resist this dishonesty. This internal revolt manifests as guilt, anxiety, or a profound sense of unease, pushing us toward confronting the truth. Authenticity begins with honest self-reflection.

Space for Self Contemplation Notes !!!

Quote 5:

"Love is to embrace, not to please!"

True love is characterized by acceptance and unconditional embrace, rather than a constant effort to conform to another's expectations or desires. It's about valuing authenticity and fostering a space where individuals can be their true selves without fear of judgment. This perspective suggests that pleasing others at the cost of one's own identity is not genuine love. Love flourishes when both individuals feel truly seen and accepted.

Space for Self Contemplation Notes !!!

Quote 6:

"No matter how much light the moon receives from the sun, it never glows on its own ... so is true with a negative mind!"

Just as the moon reflects light but generates none of its own, a negative mind, even when surrounded by positivity, fails to truly radiate. It can absorb external influences but struggles to create its own internal light or joy. This highlights the self-limiting nature of negativity, emphasizing that true brilliance and inner peace must be cultivated from within, not merely mirrored from external sources. A positive mindset is essential for a genuine inner glow.

Space for Self Contemplation Notes !!!

Quote 7:

"Fools always act to be smart, don't disturb them... Enjoy the Circus!"

This quote suggests that individuals who lack genuine wisdom or intelligence often compensate by pretending to be clever or knowledgeable. It advises against engaging with or correcting such behavior, as it's often a futile exercise. Instead, it encourages a detached observation, viewing their antics as a form of entertainment. This perspective promotes conserving energy by not getting drawn into unproductive arguments or attempts to enlighten those unwilling to learn.

Space for Self Contemplation Notes !!!

Quote 8:

"Your intent drives you to failure or success eventually!"

The underlying intention behind our actions is a powerful determinant of our ultimate outcomes. It's not just about the effort or the strategy, but the pureness and direction of our will. A genuine, positive intent, even amidst setbacks, fosters resilience and guides towards success. Conversely, a flawed or negative intent, even with apparent temporary gains, often leads to eventual failure. Our deepest motivations shape our destiny.

Space for Self Contemplation Notes !!!

Section 2:

Navigating Relationships

Insights on Connection & Honesty

Quote 9:

"A warship is tested in high seas, so are you in challenges, cowards who abandon it become jokes!"

This quote draws a powerful parallel between a warship proving its strength in turbulent waters and individuals revealing their true character during adversity. Just as a ship abandoning its mission in a storm is deemed a failure, those who shy away from life's challenges are seen as lacking courage. It emphasizes that true mettle and resilience are forged and displayed precisely when faced with difficulties, not when life is smooth sailing. Facing challenges with fortitude earns respect, while evasion invites disdain.

Space for Self Contemplation Notes !!!

Quote 10: "

Self-respect is tested in challenges, courage is tested in acknowledging mistakes!"

This quote delineates two critical aspects of character: self-respect and courage, and how they are revealed. Self-respect isn't merely about valuing oneself but about upholding one's principles and dignity when faced with difficult situations. Similarly, true courage isn't the absence of fear but the strength to admit errors and take responsibility. Both are profoundly tested and proven not in comfort, but amidst adversity and self-reflection.

Space for Self Contemplation Notes !!!

Quote 11:

"Challenges are gateways to wonderful opportunities!!"

This optimistic quote reframes difficulties not as roadblocks, but as essential openings to new possibilities. Every challenge, by forcing us to think differently, adapt, and grow, inherently presents a chance to discover untapped potential or unforeseen solutions. It encourages a mindset where obstacles are viewed as catalysts for innovation and advancement, leading to exciting new paths. Embrace difficulties as invitations to significant breakthroughs.

Space for Self Contemplation Notes !!!

"Excuses, Reasons OR Purpose, Passion... You find what you focus on!"

This quote highlights the power of focus in shaping our reality and actions. We can choose to dwell on justifications for inaction (excuses, reasons) or be driven by a clear objective and strong emotion (purpose, passion). What we consistently give our attention to—be it obstacles or aspirations—will ultimately define our path and outcomes. This emphasizes the importance of intentional focus to achieve meaningful results.

Space for Self Contemplation Notes !!!

Quote 13:

"Need drives priority... otherwise it's just excuses!"

This quote asserts that genuine necessity is the primary force that establishes true priorities in our lives. When something is genuinely needed, we find the motivation and resources to address it, making it a top concern. Conversely, if something is repeatedly postponed or ignored, it often reveals a lack of true necessity, despite any reasons given. This suggests that without real need, justifications often turn into mere excuses, highlighting the difference between genuine commitment and mere pretense.

Space for Self Contemplation Notes !!!

Quote 14:

"A student with a good attitude can learn from a poor mentor, but even the best mentor cannot make a poor attitude student learn!"

This quote powerfully highlights the paramount importance of a positive attitude in the learning process. It suggests that a receptive and eager learner can extract value even from less-than-ideal guidance, demonstrating an intrinsic drive for knowledge. However, a student lacking the right disposition, despite having access to superior teaching, will fail to absorb anything. This underscores that true education is an internal act of willingness, not merely an external transfer of information.

Space for Self Contemplation Notes !!!

"We can grow or ruin self, it's all about maturity!"

This quote emphasizes that personal development and self-destruction are largely determined by one's level of maturity. Mature individuals make choices that foster growth, learning, and well-being, even when challenging. Conversely, immaturity often leads to impulsive, self-sabotaging decisions that hinder progress and cause harm. It suggests that maturity is the key differentiator in whether we build ourselves up or tear ourselves down through our actions.

Space for Self Contemplation Notes !!!

Quote 16:

"The Challenges, yes! They make success taste sweeter... face them with passion!"

This quote celebrates the transformative power of challenges, asserting that difficulties enhance the value and satisfaction of achievement. Overcoming obstacles with dedication not only builds character but also amplifies the joy and appreciation of success. It's a call to embrace adversity not with dread, but with an enthusiastic spirit, knowing that the struggle itself enriches the ultimate triumph. Passionately confronting challenges leads to more profound victories.

Space for Self Contemplation Notes !!!

Section 3:

Embracing Challenges

Perspectives on Resilience & Growth

Quote 17:

"If you want to live forever, keep learning, keep inventing solutions!"

This quote offers a metaphorical path to immortality through continuous intellectual and practical engagement. It suggests that staying relevant, impactful, and vibrant in life isn't about physical longevity, but about the ceaseless pursuit of knowledge and the active creation of solutions. By constantly learning and innovating, we ensure our ideas and contributions live on, making us timeless. A spirit of perpetual inquiry fuels an endless life.

Space for Self Contemplation Notes !!!

"Once is a mistake, twice is a weakness but then it's a deliberate well thought choice... Act decisively here!"

This quote offers a sharp progression in understanding repeated errors. The first instance of an error can be attributed to a simple mistake. A repetition might indicate a weakness in execution or understanding. However, continuing the same error beyond that points to a conscious, often deliberate, decision. It urges decisive action at this critical juncture, whether to change the approach or fully accept the consequences, as further repetition becomes a choice rather than an accident.

Space for Self Contemplation Notes !!!

Quote 19:

"Life is not an evergreen garden, but sometimes a battlefield ...
it's all about the survival of the fittest, not the cutest!"

This quote presents a stark, realistic view of life, contrasting a perpetually pleasant existence with periods of intense struggle. It emphasizes that life often demands a Darwinian survival instinct, where adaptability, strength, and resilience are paramount. The notion of "survival of the fittest" here refers to mental and emotional fortitude, rather than superficial charm or appearance. It's a call to be prepared for harsh realities and to develop the inner toughness needed to thrive.

Space for Self Contemplation Notes !!!

Quote 20:

"Leadership is... seeding, nurturing confidence and passion to excel!"

This quote defines effective leadership not by authority or command, but by its ability to cultivate vital internal qualities within others. True leaders are those who inspire belief in oneself (confidence) and ignite a fervent desire for excellence (passion). Their role is to empower individuals, providing the fertile ground and sustained encouragement necessary for them to grow, thrive, and ultimately achieve their highest potential. It's a transformative, growth-oriented approach to guiding people.

Space for Self Contemplation Notes !!!

Quote 21:

"The genetic error in humans is that they believe they can keep making excuses and escape always!"

This quote highlights a common human fallacy: the tendency to perpetually rationalize inaction or failure through excuses, with the naive belief that consequences can always be evaded. It suggests this is a fundamental flaw in thinking, leading to a cycle of missed opportunities and stagnation. This "error" prevents genuine self-improvement and accountability, perpetuating a state of unfulfilled potential by avoiding responsibility. True

---

Space for Self Contemplation Notes !!!

Quote 22:

"Confusion spoils opportunity, comfort weakens it, and greed destroys it forever!"

This quote traces the destructive path of an opportunity through three psychological pitfalls. Confusion leads to inaction, letting the opportunity spoil. Comfort breeds complacency, weakening the drive to pursue it. Ultimately, unchecked greed can cause one to overreach or make unethical choices, destroying the opportunity beyond repair. It serves as a cautionary tale against internal states that undermine potential.

Space for Self Contemplation Notes !!!

"A passionate person always radiates... possibilities and ideas. Whereas a deadwood simply kills time and hides behind excuses!"

This quote vividly contrasts the dynamic energy of a passionate individual with the stagnant nature of a "deadwood." A person driven by passion naturally generates enthusiasm, innovative thoughts, and sees endless potential, inspiring those around them. In stark opposition, someone lacking passion becomes unproductive, merely passing time and avoiding responsibility through a facade of excuses. It underscores that passion is the engine of creativity and progress, while its absence leads to stagnation and avoidance.

Space for Self Contemplation Notes !!!

Quote 24:

"A true friend will sacrifice relationship by giving blunt feedback... rather than serving your ego with sweet poison!!"

This powerful quote defines true friendship by its willingness to prioritize growth over comfort. A genuine friend, concerned for your well-being, will offer honest, even harsh, criticism when needed, risking temporary discomfort or even strain on the relationship. This is contrasted with those who flatter or agree simply to maintain harmony, subtly damaging growth with insincere praise. The ultimate act of friendship is tough love that fosters improvement, not superficial appeasement.

Space for Self Contemplation Notes !!!

"Mistakes and illness, if ignored, only lead to pain & regret!"

This quote draws a parallel between neglecting errors and neglecting one's health, highlighting that both, if left unaddressed, will inevitably lead to negative consequences. Just as ignoring symptoms of illness allows a condition to worsen, avoiding accountability for mistakes prevents learning and perpetuates negative patterns. Both require prompt attention, honest assessment, and corrective action to prevent greater suffering and remorse. Proactive engagement is key to avoiding prolonged pain.

Space for Self Contemplation Notes !!!

Section 4:

Purpose & Drive

On Intent, Action & Opportunity

Quote 26:

"Your Character is reflected in the choices and compromises you made!"

This quote profoundly states that one's true character is not defined by aspirations or intentions alone, but by the tangible decisions and concessions made throughout life. Every choice, especially those involving difficult trade-offs, reveals underlying values, integrity, and priorities. It's in these real-world actions, rather than mere words, that the essence of a person's character is truly laid bare for all to see. Our decisions are the truest testament to who we are.

Space for Self Contemplation Notes !!!

"If the chair of care is not valued .... then please let them stand in queue!"

This quote uses a powerful metaphor to convey the importance of reciprocity and valuing effort in relationships. If someone's genuine care, attention, or dedicated effort is not appreciated or is taken for granted, then that care should be withheld. It implies that such individuals should experience the absence of that care, learning its value by having to wait or seek it elsewhere. It's a statement about respecting boundaries and demanding appreciation for one's contributions.

Space for Self Contemplation Notes !!!

"Hypocrisy has killed more relationships than cheating!"

This quote makes a strong assertion about the corrosive nature of hypocrisy in relationships. While cheating involves a direct betrayal of trust, hypocrisy—the pretense of virtues or beliefs one does not possess—erodes the very foundation of authenticity and genuine connection. It creates an environment of deceit and falsehood, making true intimacy impossible. The sustained dishonesty of hypocrisy often proves more damaging to bonds than a single act of infidelity, as it undermines trust at a deeper, systemic level.

Space for Self Contemplation Notes !!!

Quote 29:

"With every act of foolish selfishness exposed... a door is closed forever!"

This quote suggests that each instance of self-serving and ill-conceived selfishness, when brought to light, permanently damages opportunities or relationships. It implies that such actions reveal a fundamental flaw in character that, once seen, cannot be unseen or easily forgiven. The "door closed forever" signifies a loss of trust, respect, or access to future possibilities that were once open. It serves as a strong warning against the enduring negative consequences of selfish behavior.

Space for Self Contemplation Notes !!!

Quote 30:

"If you are not someone's morning, then don't make them your evening!"

This metaphorical quote speaks to the intensity and timing of one's presence in another's life. If you aren't a significant, positive start to their day or life ("morning"), then don't impose yourself as a burden or a problematic end ("evening"). It suggests respecting boundaries and understanding your impact, advising against becoming a source of stress or discomfort if you are not a source of joy or positive engagement. Be mindful of the energy you bring to others.

Space for Self Contemplation Notes !!!

Quote 31:

"Your true character is at its best displayed, when you have nothing to lose"

This quote suggests that genuine character is most authentically revealed when external pressures or potential losses are absent. When there are no consequences to fear—no reputation to uphold, no gain to protect—a person's intrinsic values and true nature come to the forefront. It implies that self-interest or social expectations can often mask one's real self, which is only truly unmasked when the stakes are removed. This reveals unadulterated actions.

Space for Self Contemplation Notes !!!

Quote 32:

"The best reply to critics is an evergreen SMILE and eventually a Grand Success!"

This quote offers a powerful and resilient strategy for dealing with criticism and detractors. Instead of engaging in arguments or defending oneself verbally, maintaining a calm, positive demeanor (an "evergreen smile") is advised. Ultimately, the most undeniable and effective rebuttal comes from achieving significant success, which silences critics through irrefutable results. It's a call to let actions and achievements speak louder than words.

Space for Self Contemplation Notes !!!

Quote 33:

"At what cost ??.... if it's money, immaterial. If Time, Significant. But if it's Self Respect.... It's Degrading Regret Forever You Will be left with!"

This quote urges a critical evaluation of the true cost of our decisions, emphasizing that not all costs are equal. While financial costs might be recoverable ("immaterial"), the expenditure of time is precious and irreplaceable ("significant"). However, the ultimate and most damaging cost is the compromise of one's self-respect. This leads to a permanent, debilitating sense of regret and degradation, highlighting self-respect as the most invaluable asset.

Space for Self Contemplation Notes !!!

Section 5:

The Essence of Character

Wisdom on Integrity & Value

Quote 34:

"At a traffic signal, you find both beggars and sellers.. what differentiates them is Self Respect and Confidence!"

This quote observes a common urban scene to highlight a profound difference in human agency and character. While both beggars and sellers are seeking something, the seller, even in humble circumstances, operates with a degree of self-respect and confidence by offering value in exchange. The beggar, conversely, relies on pity. This illustrates that true dignity and empowerment stem from an internal sense of worth and the belief in one's ability to contribute, regardless of external status.

Space for Self Contemplation Notes !!!

"Average Thoughts, Love for Comfort, Sympathy Hungry ... are indicators of a weak mentality and untrustworthy character"

This quote identifies three interconnected traits that signal a detrimental character. A preference for average thinking indicates a lack of intellectual ambition. A deep love for comfort suggests an aversion to effort and challenge, hindering growth. Being "sympathy hungry" points to a manipulative tendency, seeking attention and pity rather than genuine connection. Together, these traits paint a picture of an individual lacking resilience, integrity, and true strength, making them unreliable.

Space for Self Contemplation Notes !!!

Quote 36:

"If your choice is not in sync or better than your own values...
it's a mentally degrading blunder!"

This quote emphasizes the critical importance of aligning one's decisions with one's core personal values. When a choice contradicts or falls short of one's ethical standards, it leads to internal conflict and a diminishing of self-respect. Such actions, though seemingly external, cause profound psychological harm, eroding one's sense of integrity and authenticity. It warns that compromising on values is a mentally damaging mistake that leads to deep regret and a weakening of character.

Space for Self Contemplation Notes !!!

Quote 37:

"Our image is a by-product of our actions, casual acts impact it most!"

This quote highlights that one's reputation or public image is not solely built on grand gestures or deliberate presentations, but is significantly shaped by everyday, seemingly insignificant actions. It suggests that consistency in small, unconscious behaviors often reveals true character and leaves a lasting impression. These "casual acts," because they are unfiltered, often speak louder than intentional efforts to project a certain image, demonstrating that authenticity is key to a positive reputation.

Space for Self Contemplation Notes !!!

Quote 38:

"If you can't demonstrate, you are simply faking it!"

This quote sharply asserts that true understanding or capability is proven through action and demonstration, not mere words or claims. If one is unable to practically apply or show what they profess to know or believe, their assertion lacks authenticity and is simply a facade. It's a direct challenge to hypocrisy and intellectual dishonesty, emphasizing that genuine mastery is always accompanied by observable evidence. Action speaks louder than empty claims.

Space for Self Contemplation Notes !!!

Quote 39:

"Fakeness is short-lived, but ruins credibility forever!"

This quote warns about the transient nature of deceit and its devastating long-term impact on one's reputation. While a false front or dishonest act might offer temporary benefits or concealment, it inevitably crumbles under scrutiny. Once exposed, such insincerity completely erodes trust and makes it incredibly difficult to regain credibility, leaving a lasting stain on one's character. Authenticity, though harder, is the only sustainable path to respect.

Space for Self Contemplation Notes !!!

Quote 40:

"Confidence makes you a class apart!"

This quote emphasizes the transformative power of self-assurance in distinguishing individuals. Confidence isn't just about belief in one's abilities; it radiates an aura of capability and presence that sets one apart from the crowd. It enables bold action, clear communication, and an unwavering demeanor, earning respect and inspiring others. True confidence elevates a person beyond mere competence, making them truly remarkable and impactful.

Space for Self Contemplation Notes !!!

Quote 41:

"Karan lied, Duryodhan cheated, whereas courageous Arjun won the war without compromising on values... that's Guru Dakshina!"

This quote draws a profound moral lesson from the Mahabharata, contrasting characters who resorted to deceit with one who upheld integrity. Karan's and Duryodhan's actions, despite their power, were marred by dishonesty and unethical means. In contrast, Arjun's victory, achieved through courage and adherence to principles, is presented as the ultimate "Guru Dakshina" (tribute to a teacher). It implies that true success and honor are found in virtuous conduct, not in winning at any cost, thereby honoring the lessons of righteousness.

Space for Self Contemplation Notes !!!

"Suspense is amazing, your well-wishers feel excited whereas adversaries experience fear!"

This quote highlights the dual nature of suspense, particularly in competitive or challenging situations. For those who support you ("well wishers"), suspense creates thrilling anticipation and hope for a positive outcome, fueling their excitement. Conversely, for opponents ("adversaries"), the same uncertainty breeds anxiety and fear of your potential success. It underscores how the perception of an unfolding situation can evoke vastly different emotional responses depending on one's alignment.

Space for Self Contemplation Notes !!!

Section 6:

Cultivating Abundance

Reflections on Mindset & Leadership

Quote 43:

"Hypocrisy serves none, exposes the one!"

This quote succinctly captures the futility and self-destructive nature of hypocrisy. By pretending to be something one is not, the hypocrite ultimately deceives no one but themselves in the long run. The facade eventually crumbles, exposing their true character and integrity. Thus, hypocrisy serves no genuine purpose, instead leading to the revelation of one's own deceit and a loss of credibility. Authenticity is the only sustainable path to respect.

Space for Self Contemplation Notes !!!

Quote 44:

"Be deserving... instead of expecting!"

This quote shifts the focus from passive hope to active effort and merit. It encourages individuals to concentrate on cultivating the qualities, skills, and contributions that make them worthy of success, recognition, or desired outcomes. Instead of merely waiting for things to happen, it advocates for proactive self-improvement and diligent work, knowing that genuine deservingness naturally attracts positive results. Earn your rewards, don't just anticipate them.

Space for Self Contemplation Notes !!!

Quote 45:

"The cost of playing safe & selfish is image, a very costly mistake eventually!"

This quote warns against the deceptive allure of prioritizing personal safety and self-interest above all else. While such an approach might seem expedient in the short term, it ultimately erodes one's reputation and public perception. The perceived lack of courage or willingness to contribute negatively impacts how others view and trust you. This "costly mistake" of a tarnished image often outweighs any temporary gains from selfishness, leading to long-term regret.

Space for Self Contemplation Notes !!!

Quote 46:

"To miss is average, Cherish the memories!"

It's a natural human tendency to "miss" people who are important to us, whether they are absent, distant, or no longer with us. However, simply dwelling on their absence is a common, even average, response. A more enriching approach is to actively cherish the beautiful memories we've created with them. By focusing on these positive recollections, we transform simple remembrance into a source of gratitude and lasting joy.

Space for Self Contemplation Notes !!!

Quote 47:

"Memories are awesome... Thus, we never forget or never forgive!"

This quote highlights the powerful and enduring nature of memories, particularly in their ability to preserve both positive and negative experiences. It suggests that the vividness of recollection means we can neither truly "forget" significant events (good or bad) nor fully "forgive" deep harms in the sense of erasing them from our consciousness. While forgiveness can occur, the memory of the event itself remains, shaping us. It underscores the lasting impact of experiences on our psyche.

Space for Self Contemplation Notes !!!

Quote 48:

"Sunset never happens, it's the earth that makes us feel so... Life is never difficult, it's our attitude that makes us believe so!"

This profound quote uses the optical illusion of a sunset to make a powerful point about perspective. Just as the sun isn't truly setting but our planet is rotating, life's inherent difficulties are often less about external circumstances and more about our internal mindset. It suggests that a negative or fearful attitude can magnify challenges, making life seem harder than it truly is. A shift in perspective can transform perceived hardship into manageable experiences.

Space for Self Contemplation Notes !!!

Quote 49:

"The worst form of blindness is... failing to notice how blessed you are!"

This quote identifies a profound spiritual and emotional blindness: the inability to recognize and appreciate the blessings already present in one's life. It suggests that focusing solely on perceived lacks or desires prevents one from seeing the abundance that surrounds them. This form of blindness leads to discontentment, regardless of external circumstances, and is considered the "worst" because it prevents inner peace and gratitude. True vision involves recognizing one's inherent fortune.

Space for Self Contemplation Notes !!!

Quote 50:

"Abundance Devalues, Limited adds Value... Eklavya learnt from an idol, that the best students failed to learn from Guru!"

This quote presents a counter-intuitive view on value, suggesting that scarcity can sometimes enhance appreciation and drive. The first part implies that when things are too abundant, their value diminishes (e.g., unlimited access reduces appreciation). The example of Eklavya highlights how intense desire and self-directed learning from a limited "resource" (an idol) can lead to mastery, surpassing those who had direct access to a "Guru" but lacked similar drive. It underscores the power of internal motivation and focused effort over mere access to resources.

Space for Self Contemplation Notes !!!

About the Author

Paremvir Malik is a keen observer of life, an insightful thinker, and the voice behind "My Blissful Experiences with Life!" He is a strategic HR leader and passionate mentor with over 15 years of comprehensive experience, having driven HR scale-up across diverse Indian, European, and American MNCs, along with DeepTech Startups. As an ethics-driven, results-oriented HR leader, Paremvir's professional journey offers a unique perspective on human dynamics, resilience, and the power of values in both personal and organizational contexts.

His strong academic foundation includes a Masters in Labour Law & Labour Welfare from Symbiosis Society's Law College, Pune; a PGDM in Personnel Management & Human Resources from the Indian Institute of Modern Management, Pune; and a Bachelor of Arts (Defence & Strategic Studies) from Bhonsala Military College, Pune University.

Demonstrating early leadership and a commitment to community, Paremvir holds the distinction of being the Youngest Founder President of a Sport NGO – Ozar Gymkhana, Nasik, Maharashtra, INDIA.

His dedication to mentorship and innovation has garnered significant recognition. He has been featured as a Star Mentor & HR Advisor by Topmate.io on a billboard at Times Square, New

York, USA. Furthermore, as a Mentor of Change for Atal Innovation Mission (NITI AAYOG, Govt. of India), he has been recognized as 'GEM OF MENTOR INDIA' and 'Exemplary Mentor of Change' for his substantial contributions to innovation and entrepreneurship, having mentored over 3000 students.

Through a collection of powerful quotes and reflections, Paremvir shares a deep understanding of self-awareness, human relationships, and the path to inner contentment. The wisdom encapsulated in this book is a testament to a journey of embracing challenges, fostering resilience, and striving for integrity and purpose. Paremvir's work encourages readers to explore their inner compass, navigate life with honesty, and cultivate a mindset of abundance and growth. This book is a heartfelt invitation to discover the bliss that emerges when one truly listens to the soul and lives in alignment with core values.